FRIDAY
NIGHT
COCKTAILS

FRIDAY

52 Drinks

NIGHT

to Welcome Your Weekend

COCKTAILS

BY A.J. DEAN

Library of Congress Cataloging-in-Publication Data available.
ISBN: 978-1-68555-486-6
Ebook ISBN: 978-1-68555-670-9
Library of Congress Control Number: 2023930406

Printed using Forest Stewardship Council certified stock from sustainably managed forests.

Manufactured in China.

Design by AJ Hansen.

Photo credits:
By AJ Hansen, copyright © 2023: pages 18, 22, 32, 34, 40, 43, 44, 52, 54, 60, 66, 74, 76, 81, 87, 88, 91, 95, 99, 110, 127, 135, 137, 143, 147

By Katelyn Perry from Unsplash: pages 2, 4, 6, 12, 46, 70, 78, 120, 148

Licensed from Unsplash: pages, 25, 26, 39, 58, 116, 123, 124, 144

Licensed from Shutterstock: pages 14, 21, 29, 48, 50, 56, 64, 73, 82, 96, 103, 104, 108, 114, 119, 131, 132, 138

10 9 8 7 6 5 4 3 2 1

The Collective Book Studio®
Oakland, California
www.thecollectivebook.studio

Page 152 constitutes a continuation of the copyright page.

To Jackson, whose never-ending pursuit of just the right elixir at just the right time will take him far in the world.

CONTENTS

Introduction 8

Autumn 12

Winter 46

Spring 78

Summer 116

Index 150

a tiny bit about cocktail history ...

Prior to the 1800s as sailors traveled the globe they discovered and happily embraced the spirits made by locals. Think of rum in the Caribbean. Along with spirits, they usually found varieties of fruits as well as spices. When the sailors blended these ingredients together, "punch" was born. These early punches contained alcohol, sugar, water, citrus, and spices.

A punch was great for a large gathering; not so great for an individual who just wanted to have a drink. In the early 1800s, the communal punch bowl, which the sailors brought home with them, began to be replaced by single serving-size drinks. Further, the citrus and spices were gradually replaced by bitters, which were an available (and popular) alternative.

Bitters have been around since the ancient Egyptians. The thing about bitters is, well, they're bitter. Still, people reasoned, anything that tastes so unpleasant must be good for you, right? Yes. Bitters were "prescribed" as a cure for everything from indigestion to malaria. And because of this seeming medicinal use, the concoctions largely

fell under the purview of pharmacists ("druggists" in North America). Bitters are historically made from bark, herbs, fruit peels, roots, botanicals, and other ingredients (all of which are added to a flavorless alcohol).

Which brings us to the modern cocktail. Well, almost. The first use of the word "cocktail" appeared in a newspaper article in 1806. That simple recipe called for alcohol, sugar, water, and bitters. As the article stated, a cocktail will make "the heart flout and bold, at the same time that it fuddles the head." It would take another fifty-plus years for the first cocktail—the Sazerac—to arrive on the scene.

* * *

The key to a delicious cocktail is balance. With a little understanding of the roles of the main components—alcohol, water, sugar, bitters—you can begin to experiment on your own. Like the French 75 cocktail (gin, lemon juice, simple syrup, sparkling wine)? Why not try grapefruit juice in place of the lemon? Or make the same recipe but use different gins?

The cocktails in this book are meant to be easy to make and come with many variations to encourage YOU. BE BOLD. EXPERIMENT.

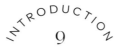

a tiny bit about barware ...

Cocktail shaker

There are two common types of shakers: cobbler and Boston. A cobbler shaker includes a cup basin with a detachable top, measuring cap, and strainer. A Boston shaker uses two weighted, metal cups that seal together to quickly mix multiple drinks.

Mixing glass

As the older brother to the cocktail shaker, the mixing glass serves a similar purpose, though it generally produces a less-diluted cocktail. A mixing glass requires the use of a strainer and a bar spoon.

Strainer

The most common strainer is the Hawthorne strainer, which is all you'll need for most cocktails. If you want a finer strain, you can use a fine-mesh sieve.

Bar spoon

While any spoon will technically work for mixing a cocktail, the traditional bar spoon has an extra long handle to keep the bartenders fingers away from the drink and give extra mobility when stirring.

Jigger or measured shot glass

A jigger is a volumetric measuring tool designed specifically for cocktail mixing. They note common measurements and come in several sizes.

Citrus juicer

The cocktails in this book recommend the use of fresh citrus juice whenever possible. A citrus juicer is an easy-to-use and nearly irreplaceable tool when extracting fresh lime, lemon, or orange juice at home.

a tiny bit
about glassware . . .

Cocktail glasses come in all shapes and sizes. While each recipe notes the traditional glassware used, the real star of the show will always be the drink itself. Below is a list of the glassware in this book, but you can pour your Friday night cocktail into any vessel you choose.

Highball	Hurricane	Daiquiri
Lowball	Wineglass	Mug
Martini	Champagne flute	Copper mule mug
Coupe		Julep cup
Margarita	Beer glass	

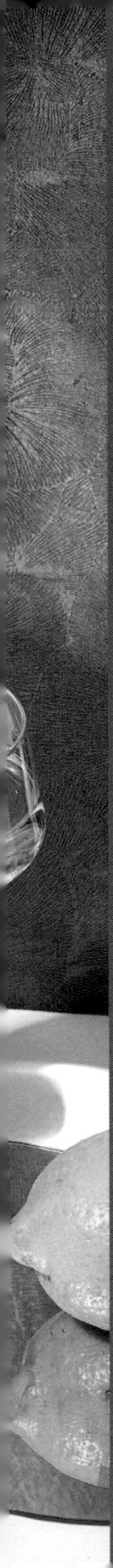

SEPTEMBER

Amaretto Sour 15

Pear & Elderflower Sparkler 19

Sazerac 20

Chocolate Old Fashioned 23

Vesper Martini 24

Martinez 27

Scofflaw 28

Pumpkin Pie Cocktail 33

The Last Word 34

Negroni Sbagliato 38

Applejack Sour 41

Kir Royale 42

Sidecar 45

NOVEMBER

AMARETTO SOUR

The lovely thing about the Amaretto Sour is that you can make an individual drink or pre-batch a pitcher for a gathering. Because it's so easy to make, it's perfect for sipping with a friend or two or as a nightcap after a long week.

GLASS: Lowball	GARNISH: Dried Orange Wheel

1½ oz/45 ml amaretto liqueur

1 oz/30 ml lemon juice, freshly squeezed

1 oz/30 ml simple syrup

Dried orange wheel, for garnish (see Tip, page 17)

In a cocktail shaker, add the amaretto, lemon juice, and simple syrup. Add ice and shake until chilled. Strain into a cocktail glass with ice and garnish with a dried orange wheel.

VARIATION: *Check out the version crafted by bartender Jeffrey Morganthaler, in Portland, Oregon. His version adds ¾ oz (22 ml) cask-proof bourbon (60% ABV or higher) as well as ½ oz (15 ml) egg white (see Tip page 85) to give the drink a silky texture. Once again, combine all ingredients in a cocktail shaker, first without the ice, and shake. Add ice and shake once more to chill before serving.*

Dried Citrus

If you ever find yourself with leftover citrus and nothing to do with the rest, consider drying it for future drinks.

Preheat your oven to 200 degrees F. Line a baking tray with parchment paper and set aside.

Using a sharp knife or mandolin, cut the citrus into slices no more than ¼-inch wide. Place the citrus on the prepared tray and bake for 4–5 hours. Halfway through the baking time, flip each citrus wheel.

Dried citrus can be stored in a moisture-free container for up to a year.

PEAR & ELDERFLOWER SPARKLER

In autumn and early winter, when pears become abundant in local markets, celebrate the season with a delicious sparkling drink. Simply put, this is a fun cocktail that's quick and easy to make.

GLASS: Coupe		GARNISH: Pear slices
½ oz/15 ml elderflower liqueur ½ oz/15 ml lemon juice, freshly squeezed		1 oz/30 ml pear juice 3 oz/90 ml prosecco Pear slices, for garnish

In a mixing glass filled with ice, add the elderflower liqueur, lemon juice, and pear juice. Stir until well chilled. Strain into a cocktail glass and top with prosecco. Garnish with pear slices.

VARIATION: **FRENCH PEAR MARTINI.** *In a mixing glass filled with ice, add 1½ oz (45 ml) pear vodka, 1½ oz (45 ml) elderflower liqueur, and 3 oz (90 ml) prosecco. Stir until well chilled. Strain into a cocktail glass and garnish with pear slices.*

AUTUMN

SAZERAC

|

Historians agree that the Sazerac is the oldest cocktail in America, though its exact origin remains a mystery. It may be that the earliest version—a medicinal concoction made in the mid-1800s by a New Orleans druggist named Peychaud—included the cognac named Sazerac de Forge et Fils.

GLASS: Lowball		GARNISH: Lemon twist
¼ oz/7 ml absinthe, to rinse 1 tsp sugar 4 dashes Peychaud's bitters		2 oz/60 ml rye whiskey Lemon twist, for garnish

In a cocktail glass, add the absinthe and swirl to coat the inside of the glass. Discard any excess and set the glass aside. In a mixing glass filled with ice, add the sugar, bitters, and a few drops of water and mix until well combined. Add the whiskey and stir until chilled. Strain into the prepared cocktail glass and garnish with a lemon twist.

VARIATION: *To pay homage to the French brandy used in the original Sazerac cocktail, combine 1 oz (30 ml) rye whiskey with 1 oz (30 ml) cognac. This variation accentuates the licorice flavor while keeping the overall cocktail balanced and bold.*

CHOCOLATE OLD FASHIONED

(Wait . . . What? Isn't this a variation on a classic?) *The early cocktails of the 1800s were simple affairs— sugar, water, bitters, and alcohol. When bartenders began to experiment with other ingredients, customers balked! They asked to just have their drinks made the old-fashioned way.* (So, why fix something that ain't broken? Ah . . . chocolate.)

GLASS: Lowball	GARNISH: Grated chocolate
1 tsp sugar 3 dashes chocolate bitters 2 oz/60 ml bourbon	Chocolate, grated, for garnish

In a cocktail glass, add the sugar, bitters, and a dash of water and stir until combined. Then add the bourbon. Add a large ice cube and stir gently. Garnish with grated chocolate.

VARIATION: *Okay, here's how to make a classic* **OLD FASHIONED.** *In a mixing glass, add 1 tsp sugar, 1 tsp water, and 3 dashes bitters and stir until the sugar is dissolved. Fill with ice and add 2 oz (60 ml) bourbon. Stir until well chilled. Strain into a cocktail glass and garnish with an orange twist.*

VESPER MARTINI

Readers were introduced to Vesper Lynd in Casino Royale, *the 1953 James Bond novel by Ian Fleming. Long story short: Boy meets girl, boy and girl fall in love, girl dies tragically, boy carries a torch for years. Fleming included veiled references to Bond's heartache in several subsequent books. It's only fitting that Bond would create a cocktail in her name.*

GLASS: Coupe or martini	GARNISH: Lemon twist
2 oz/60 ml gin ⅔ oz/20 ml vodka	⅓ oz/10 ml Lillet Blanc Lemon twist, for garnish

In a mixing glass filled with ice, add the gin, vodka, and Lillet Blanc. Stir until well chilled. Strain into a cocktail glass. Rub a lemon rind over the rim of the glass and garnish with a lemon twist.

VARIATION: *In 1987 the makers of Lillet Blanc reformulated their aperitif, leaving lovers of this martini variation with only an approximation of the original Kina Lillet flavor. To better match the cocktail from Fleming's era, substitute Cocchi Americano, which is slightly sweeter than Lillet Blanc.*

MARTINEZ

The drink that became the martini. While all gin-based cocktails will have a different character depending on which gin you use, the Martinez in particular is great to experiment with. On the one hand, the drink can be bracing in flavor; on the other, it can be citrusy or floral.

GLASS: Coupe	GARNISH: Orange twist

1½ oz/45 ml gin

1½ oz/45 ml sweet vermouth

¼ oz/7 ml maraschino liqueur (see Tip, page 37)

2 dashes Angostura bitters

Orange twist, for garnish

In a mixing glass filled with ice, add the gin, vermouth, maraschino liqueur, and bitters. Stir until well chilled. Strain into a cocktail glass and garnish with an orange twist.

VARIATION: **HANKY PANKY.** *In a mixing glass filled with ice, add 1½ oz (45 ml) gin, 1½ oz (45 ml) sweet vermouth, and ½ tsp fernet. Stir until well chilled. Strain into a cocktail glass and garnish with an orange twist.*

SCOFFLAW

A drink born during Prohibition, the Scofflaw was named for those ne'er-do-wells who happily scoffed at the law. Even as speakeasy bars sprang up across the country, it's interesting to note that the Scofflaw cocktail was actually created outside the United States, at Harry's Bar in Paris.

GLASS: Coupe	GARNISH: None

2 oz/60 ml rye whiskey

¾ oz/22 ml dry vermouth

¾ oz/22 ml/20 ml lemon juice, freshly squeezed

¾ oz/22 ml/20 ml Pomegranate Syrup (page 31)

1 dash orange bitters

In a cocktail shaker, add the whiskey, vermouth, lemon juice, Pomegranate Syrup, and bitters. Add ice and shake until chilled. Strain into a cocktail glass.

Pomegranate Syrup

Pomegranate syrup is substituted
throughout for grenadine.

16 oz/32 ml
pomegranate juice

2 cups/400 g sugar

2 Tbsp lemon juice,
freshly squeezed

In a medium saucepan over medium heat,
combine the pomegranate juice, sugar,
and lemon juice. Bring to a boil and stir
to dissolve the sugar, about 5 minutes.
Remove from heat and let cool. Store in
an airtight container. The syrup will last
about a month in the refrigerator.

PUMPKIN PIE COCKTAIL

What's better than pumpkin pie? How about a boozy pumpkin pie in a glass. Thanksgiving leftovers, anyone?

GLASS: Martini	GARNISH: Cinnamon stick
2 oz/60 ml vodka	¼ tsp pure vanilla extract
1 oz/30 ml dark rum	Pinch of pumpkin pie spice
2 Tbsp pumpkin purée	½ oz/15 ml half-and-half
1 oz/30 ml maple syrup	Cinnamon stick, for garnish

In a cocktail shaker, add the vodka, rum, pumpkin purée, maple syrup, vanilla, pumpkin pie spice, and half-and-half. Add ice and shake until chilled. Strain into a cocktail glass and garnish with a cinnamon stick.

VARIATION: *Since you have the pumpkin pie spice and pumpkin purée already at hand, try a* **PUMPKIN PIE MULE.** *In a cocktail shaker, add 2 oz (60 ml) vodka, ½ oz (15 ml) lime juice, 1 Tbsp pumpkin purée, and ¼ tsp pumpkin pie spice. Add ice and shake until chilled. Strain into a mule mug and top with 4 oz (120 ml) ginger beer. Garnish with a sprinkle of pumpkin pie spice.*

THE LAST WORD

This Prohibition-era drink was first conceived in the 1920s in Detroit. After several decades of popularity, it fell into obscurity, only to be rediscovered in the mid-2000s.

GLASS: Coupe	GARNISH: Brandied cherry
¾ oz/22 ml gin ¾ oz/22 ml maraschino liqueur (see Tip, page 37) ¾ oz/22 ml Green Chartreuse	¾ oz/22 ml lime juice, freshly squeezed Brandied cherry, for garnish

In a cocktail shaker, add the gin, maraschino liqueur, Chartreuse, and lime juice. Add ice and shake until chilled. Strain into a cocktail glass and garnish with a brandied cherry.

VARIATION: **LA ÚLTIMA PALABRA.** *In a cocktail shaker, add ¾ oz (22 ml) mezcal, ¾ oz (22 ml) maraschino liqueur, ¾ oz (22 ml) Green Chartreuse, and ¾ oz (22 ml) lime juice. Add ice and shake until chilled. Strain into a cocktail glass and garnish with a lime wheel.*

TIP

Maraschino Liqueur

Maraschino liqueur is not the same
as cherry liqueur. The latter is deep
red in color, while maraschino is clear.
Importantly, keep it refrigerated. Once
opened, the liqueur can become moldy and
start to develop off flavors if left at room
temperature.

NEGRONI SBAGLIATO

In Italian, sbagliato means "messed up" or "mistaken." History would like to tell us that, while making a classic negroni, a distracted bartender grabbed a bottle of prosecco instead of the called-for gin. History may also vary the exact details. In any event, you have a refreshing reminder that sometimes a mistake is a good thing.

GLASS: Lowball	GARNISH: Orange peel
1 oz/30 ml Campari 1 oz/30 ml sweet vermouth	1 oz/30 ml prosecco or other sparkling wine Orange peel, for garnish

Fill a cocktail glass with ice. Add the Campari and vermouth and stir to mix. Top with the prosecco—the Campari and vermouth will still be "settled" at the bottom. Garnish with an orange peel and serve with a cocktail straw.

VARIATION: *Negroni variations are vast and numerous . . . and always delicious. First, though, here's the recipe for the* **CLASSIC NEGRONI.** *In a mixing glass filled with ice, combine 1 oz (30 ml) gin, 1 oz (30 ml) Campari, and 1 oz (30 ml) sweet vermouth. Stir until well chilled. Strain into a cocktail glass and garnish with an orange peel.*

APPLEJACK SOUR

If you love the flavor of apples, you'll surely like this cocktail. Applejack is a strong liquor with a rich apple flavor—a combination of apple brandy and neutral spirits. Adjust the ratio of the applejack to the rye, depending on how much apple goodness you prefer.

GLASS: Coupe	GARNISH: Grated Nutmeg
1 oz/30 ml applejack 1 oz/30 ml rye whiskey ¼ oz/7 ml maple syrup ¾ oz/22 ml lemon juice, freshly squeezed	½ oz/15 ml orange juice, freshly squeezed 2 dashes Angostura bitters Grated nutmeg, for garnish

In a cocktail shaker, add the applejack, whiskey, maple syrup, lemon juice, orange juice, and bitters. Add ice and shake until chilled. Strain into a cocktail glass and garnish with freshly grated nutmeg.

VARIATION: *Popular in the 1920s and '30s, the* **JACK ROSE** *cocktail is an interesting take, adding grenadine. In a cocktail shaker, add 1½ oz (45 ml) applejack, ¾ oz (22 ml) lemon juice, and ½ oz (15 ml) Pomegranate Syrup (page 31). Add ice and shake until chilled. Strain into a cocktail glass and garnish with a lemon twist.*

KIR ROYALE

There's no denying that sometimes simplicity really is the best—and the Kir Royale exemplifies this perfectly. Riffing on the classic French cocktail called the Kir— crème de cassis topped with white wine—the Kir Royale simply swaps the wine with Champagne.

GLASS: Champagne flute	GARNISH: Raspberry

1 oz/30 ml black currant liqueur
6 oz/180 ml Champagne
Raspberry, for garnish

In a Champagne flute, add the black currant liqueur and top with Champagne. Garnish with a raspberry.

VARIATION: *Any berry liqueur (Chambord or crème de framboise, for example) will make an excellent Kir Royale. Just remember that the drink should not be too sweet. The role of the Champagne is to balance the sweetness.*

SIDECAR

As one of the most popular brandy-based cocktails, the Sidecar is a decided classic. While there are several ways to prepare it, here's a traditional preparation that includes a sugared rim for the glass.

GLASS: Coupe or martini	GARNISH: Lemon twist

Sugar, for the rim

Lemon wedge, for the rim

1½ oz/45 ml brandy

¾ oz/22 ml Cointreau

¾ oz/22 ml lemon juice, freshly squeezed

Lemon twist, for garnish

To prepare the cocktail glass, sprinkle sugar onto a small plate. Wipe a lemon wedge around the edge of the glass, then dip the rim into the sugar.

In a cocktail shaker, add the brandy, Cointreau, and lemon juice. Add ice and shake until chilled. Strain into a prepared cocktail glass and garnish with a lemon twist.

WINTER

Classic Manhattan   49

Rob Roy   50

Cranberry Mule   53

Clementine Wallbanger   54

Hot Toddy   57

Espresso Martini   58

Penicillin   61

French 75   64

Hot Buttered Rum   67

Dirty Martini   71

Irish Coffee   72

Boulevardier   75

Blood Orange Margarita   76

CLASSIC MANHATTAN

Because of the way its subtle bitterness couples with herbal flavors, the Manhattan has become the cocktail of choice for whiskey lovers. Traditionally, the drink is made with rye, but bourbon is a very common ingredient. Either way, you'll love the simplicity of this classic cocktail.

GLASS: Coupe	GARNISH: Brandied cherry
2 oz/60 ml rye whiskey	2 dashes Angostura bitters
1 oz/30 ml sweet vermouth	Brandied cherry, for garnish

In a mixing glass filled with ice, add the whiskey, vermouth, and bitters. Stir until well chilled. Strain into a cocktail glass and garnish with a brandied cherry.

VARIATION: *Created in 2005 by San Francisco bartender Todd Smith, the* **BLACK MANHATTAN** *is something of a brooding offspring of the classic. In a mixing glass filled with ice, add 2 oz (60 ml) rye whiskey, 1 oz (30 ml) Amaro Averna, and 1 dash each Angostura and orange bitters. Stir until well chilled. Strain into a cocktail glass and garnish with a brandied cherry.*

ROB ROY

Simply put, a Rob Roy is a Manhattan made with Scotch whisky instead of bourbon or rye. Named after the famed Scottish outlaw, it's one of the most well-known Scotch cocktails. Whether you choose a blended or single-malt Scotch, you'll likely add the Rob Roy to your standby list.

GLASS: Coupe	GARNISH: Brandied cherry

2 oz/60 ml Scotch whisky

¾ oz/22 ml sweet vermouth

2 dashes Angostura bitters

Brandied cherry, for garnish

In a mixing glass filled with ice, add the Scotch, vermouth, and bitters. Stir until well chilled. Strain into a cocktail glass and garnish with a brandied cherry.

VARIATION: *For a less-sweet drink, try a* **PERFECT ROB ROY** *cocktail. In a mixing glass filled with ice, add 2 oz (60 ml) Scotch, ½ oz (15 ml) sweet vermouth, ½ oz (15 ml) dry vermouth, and 2 dashes Angostura bitters. Stir until well chilled. Strain into a cocktail glass and garnish with a brandied cherry.*

CRANBERRY MULE

This drink has holiday spirit written all over it. It's pretty, it's tart and sweet, and you can even omit the vodka for a nonalcoholic version that's equally as tasty.

GLASS: Copper mule mug	GARNISH: Lime wheel, cranberries

2 oz/60 ml vodka

2 oz/60 ml sweetened cranberry juice

½ oz/15 ml lime juice, freshly squeezed

4 oz/120 ml ginger beer

Lime wheel, for garnish

Cranberries, for garnish

Fill a copper mule mug with ice. Add the vodka, cranberry juice, and lime juice. Stir to mix and top with ginger beer. Garnish with a lime wheel and cranberries.

VARIATION: *For a* **CRANBERRY MULE MOCKTAIL**, *leave out the vodka and double the amount of cranberry juice. You can also substitute ginger ale for the ginger beer.*

CLEMENTINE WALLBANGER

Come January, you may be wondering what to do with all those Cuties, a.k.a. clementines. They're delicious, and they're everywhere! Well, this riff on the classic Harvey Wallbanger is your rescuer. The clementine and the Galliano float, with its vanilla-anise touch, definitely raises the bar on an old standby. No more vodka and orange juice for you.

GLASS: Highball	GARNISH: Clementine slice
1¼ oz/37 ml vodka	½ oz/15 ml Galliano liqueur
3 oz/90 ml clementine juice, freshly squeezed	Clementine slice, for garnish

Fill a cocktail glass with ice. Add the vodka and clementine juice and stir to mix. Float the Galliano on top. Garnish with a clementine slice.

VARIATION: *Now that you're staring at that bottle of Galliano, wondering what to do with it . . . how about a* **GALLIANO OLD FASHIONED**? *In a mixing glass filled with ice, add 1 oz (30 ml) bourbon, 1 oz (30 ml) Galliano, and 2 dashes each Angostura and orange bitters. Stir until well chilled. Strain into a cocktail glass and garnish with an orange twist.*

HOT TODDY

This drink is simplicity at its best—hot water, whiskey or bourbon, some lemon, and spices. Oh, and a chilly evening.

GLASS: Mug		GARNISH: Lemon wheel
1 cup/240 ml boiling water 1 Tbsp lemon juice, freshly squeezed 2 tsp honey		3 whole cloves 1 cinnamon stick 2 oz/60 ml bourbon Lemon wheel, for garnish

In a mug, add the boiling water, lemon juice, honey, cloves, and cinnamon stick. Stir lightly until the honey has dissolved. Set aside and let the ingredients steep for 5 minutes. Add bourbon and stir. Garnish with a lemon wheel.

VARIATION: *For a more flavor-forward variation of this classic winter cocktail, steep a bag of black tea in the boiling water for up to 1 minute. In addition, try substituting cognac for the bourbon.*

ESPRESSO MARTINI

Credit legendary British bartender Dick Bradsell for this delicious concoction. The story he tells is that a now-famous model asked for a drink to "wake me up and f*ck me up." His solution is now considered a classic. Typically, the Espresso Martini is made with Kahlúa and topped with three coffee beans (for health, happiness, and prosperity).

GLASS: Coupe or martini	GARNISH: Coffee beans
2 oz/60 ml vodka ½ oz/15 ml coffee liqueur ¼ oz/7 ml simple syrup	1 oz/30 ml espresso, freshly brewed Coffee beans, for garnish

In a cocktail shaker, add the vodka, coffee liqueur, simple syrup, and espresso. Add ice and shake until chilled. Strain into a cocktail glass. Garnish with coffee beans floated on the top.

VARIATION: *Let's face it, not everyone has an espresso machine. Not to worry. Here's a recipe for an* **EASY ESPRESSO MARTINI**, *using store-bought cold-brew coffee. In a cocktail glass, add 2 oz (60 ml) vodka, 1 oz (30 ml) cold-brew coffee, and 1 oz (30 ml) coffee liqueur and stir to mix. Add an ice cube and serve.*

PENICILLIN

Created in 2005 by an Australian bartender named Sam Ross—he was just twenty-two and working in a bar in Manhattan, no less—this drink will almost make you want to get sick more often. (Just kidding. About getting sick, that is.) The addition of the single malt floating on top adds a smoky aroma before you taste the sweet, tart cocktail.

GLASS: Lowball		GARNISH: Candied ginger

2 oz/60 ml blended Scotch whisky

¾ oz/22 ml lemon juice, freshly squeezed

¾ oz/22 ml Ginger-Honey Syrup (page 63)

¼ oz/7 ml single malt Scotch

Candied ginger, for garnish

In a cocktail shaker, add the blended Scotch, lemon juice, and Ginger-Honey Syrup. Add ice and shake until chilled. Strain into a cocktail glass with ice and top with the single malt Scotch. Garnish with pieces of candied ginger.

Ginger-Honey Syrup

1 cup/340 g honey
4 in/10 cm piece ginger, peeled and sliced

In a small saucepan over medium heat, combine the honey, 1 cup/240 ml of water, and the ginger. Bring to a boil, then remove the pan from heat and let cool. Let the syrup steep for 30 minutes (or longer if you like a strong ginger flavor). Strain and discard the ginger. Store in an airtight container in the refrigerator for up to two weeks.

FRENCH 75

This is one boozy drink! Legend says that it harkens back to the deadly 75-millimeter guns used by the French in World War I. What fills your glass today, however, is quite different from the original 1915 Soixante-Quinze ("Seventy-Five"). Though the recipe has changed several times over the years, the French 75 still ranks in the upper echelon of cocktails, alongside the Manhattan and Old Fashioned.

GLASS: Champagne flute		GARNISH: Lemon twist
1 oz/30 ml gin ½ oz/15 ml lemon juice, freshly squeezed		½ oz/15 ml simple syrup 3 oz/90 ml Champagne Lemon twist, for garnish

In a cocktail shaker, add the gin, lemon juice, and simple syrup. Add ice and shake until chilled. Strain into a Champagne flute and top with Champagne. Garnish with a lemon twist.

VARIATION: *If you substitute vodka for the gin, you've made a* **FRENCH 76**. *Or you could try elderflower liqueur instead of the gin. But then you have a* **FRENCH 77**. *Bourbon, instead? That would be a* **FRENCH 95**.

HOT BUTTERED RUM

If you're put off by the idea of drinking butter, don't be. With a batter made from warm spices and sugar, you'll soon come to appreciate the richness and depth that is the hallmark of this cocktail comfort food.

GLASS: Mug		GARNISH: Cinnamon stick

2 oz/60 ml gold rum

1 Tbsp Buttered Rum Batter (page 69)

Boiling water, to top

Cinnamon stick, for garnish

In a mug, add the rum and batter. Fill with boiling water and stir until the batter is dissolved. Garnish with a cinnamon stick.

RECIPE

Buttered Rum Batter

There are numerous recipes for the batter, which defines this drink. (Some even call for using vanilla ice cream.) Here's an easy one:

⅔ cup/230 g dark brown sugar

½ cup/110 g unsalted butter, at room temperature

¼ cup/85 g honey

½ tsp ground cinnamon

¼ tsp ground nutmeg

⅛ tsp ground cloves

Pinch of salt

In a large bowl, combine the sugar, butter, honey, cinnamon, nutmeg, cloves, and salt and beat until smooth. Transfer to an airtight container and store in the refrigerator or, better yet, in the freezer.

DIRTY MARTINI

President Franklin Roosevelt was a big fan of the Dirty Martini and is known to have served them during his time in the White House. Still, this savory take on the classic remains controversial. But don't be offended by the eye-rolling cocktail snobs. Instead, relish the umami flavor and know that you're in storied company.

GLASS: Martini	GARNISH: Olives

2½ oz/75 ml vodka

½ oz/15 ml dry vermouth

½ oz/15 ml olive brine

Olives, for garnish

In a mixing glass filled with ice, add the vodka, vermouth, and olive brine. Stir until well chilled. Strain into a cocktail glass and garnish with olives.

VARIATION: **50/50 MARTINI.** *In a mixing glass filled with ice, add 1½ oz (45 ml) gin, 1½ oz (45 ml) dry vermouth, and 1 dash orange bitters. Stir until well chilled. Strain into a cocktail glass and garnish with a lemon twist.*

IRISH COFFEE

This legendary drink dates back to 1943 and the air base at Foynes Port, located near Limerick, Ireland. When a late-night flight on its way to New York had to turn back because of bad weather, the restaurant's bartender whipped up a special concoction for the returnees. As the story goes, a silence quickly descended over the room. The weary travelers were in awe, and a legend was born.

GLASS: Mug	GARNISH: Whipped cream

1 cup/240 ml hot coffee, freshly brewed

1 Tbsp sugar

1½ oz/45 ml Irish whiskey

1 oz/30 ml heavy cream, whipped

In a mug, add the coffee, sugar, and whiskey. Stir until the sugar is dissolved. Top with whipped cream.

VARIATION: **KENTUCKY COFFEE.** *In a mug, add 1 cup (240 ml) hot coffee, 1 Tbsp sugar, and 1½ oz (45 ml) bourbon. Stir until the sugar is dissolved. Top with whipped cream.*

BOULEVARDIER

While the gin-based Negroni is crisp, the Boulevardier is warming due to its whiskey base. It's just right for a chilly evening. Like the Negroni, the drink is typically made with equal parts bourbon, Campari, and sweet vermouth.

GLASS: Lowball		GARNISH: Orange twist

1 oz/30 ml bourbon

1 oz/30 ml Campari

1 oz/30 ml sweet vermouth

Orange twist, for garnish

In a mixing glass filled with ice, add the bourbon, Campari, and sweet vermouth. Stir until well chilled. Strain into a cocktail glass with ice and garnish with an orange twist.

VARIATION: *Feel free to add a bit more whiskey (¼ oz/7 ml) if you like your drink a little less bitter or herbal.*

BLOOD ORANGE MARGARITA

Blood orange juice adds an intense citrus flavor to this much-loved cocktail, as well as a unique blush color. If you can't find blood oranges, navel oranges make a drink that is just as tasty.

GLASS: Margarita or lowball	GARNISH: Orange wheel
2 tsp salt, for the rim 1 tsp sugar, for the rim 2 oz/60 ml tequila blanco 2 oz/60 ml blood orange juice, freshly squeezed	1 oz/30 ml lime juice, freshly squeezed 1 tsp agave nectar Blood orange wheel, for garnish (see Tip, page 17)

To prepare the cocktail glass, sprinkle the salt and sugar onto a small plate. Wipe an orange wedge around the edge of a cocktail glass, then dip the rim into the salt and sugar mixture.

In a cocktail shaker, add the tequila, blood orange juice, lime juice, and agave nectar. Add ice and shake until chilled. Strain into the prepared cocktail glass with ice and garnish with a dried blood orange wheel.

SPRING

MARCH

———————————————

Cucumber Mint Gimlet   80

Pink Lady   83

Ginger Lime Whiskey Sour   86

Cosmopolitan   89

Spicy Paloma   90

Chrysanthemum   94

Gibson Martini   97

Peach-Raspberry Bellini   98

Aviation   102

Clover Club   105

Mint Julep   108

Lavender Bee's Knees   111

Lemon Drop   114

———————————————

MAY

CUCUMBER MINT GIMLET

Something magical happens when you combine gin, lime, and a touch of sweetener. Add cucumber and mint, and you have a drink that has springtime written all over it.

GLASS: Coupe

GARNISH: Cucumber wheel, mint sprig

10 mint leaves

2 in/5 cm cucumber, peeled and quartered

½ oz/15 ml simple syrup

1 oz/30 ml lime juice, freshly squeezed

1½ oz/45 ml gin

Cucumber wheel, for garnish

Mint sprig, for garnish

In a cocktail shaker, add the mint and lightly muddle to release the mint oils. Then add the cucumber and simple syrup and continue muddling. Add the lime juice , gin, and ice and shake until chilled. Strain into a cocktail glass and garnish with a cucumber wheel and sprig of mint.

PINK LADY

Refreshing and sophisticated, the Pink Lady cocktail became a favorite of high-society women of the 1930s. Including the egg white created a silky texture that only furthered its classiness. But don't be fooled by appearances—the Pink Lady packs a punch.

GLASS: Coupe		GARNISH: Brandied cherry
1½ oz/45 ml gin ¾ oz/22 ml lemon juice, freshly squeezed ¼ oz/7 ml Pomegranate Syrup (page 31)		½ oz/15 ml applejack 1 small egg white (see Tip, page 85) Brandied cherry, for garnish

In a cocktail shaker, combine the gin, lemon juice, Pomegranate Syrup, applejack, and egg white. Shake until well combined and frothy. Add ice and shake until chilled. Strain into a cocktail glass and garnish with a brandied cherry.

VARIATION: *Adding powdered sugar with the egg white gives the foam an icing-like texture and makes the drink a touch sweeter. If this appeals to you, add 1 tsp powdered sugar along with the other ingredients.*

Egg White Foam

When adding egg white to a cocktail shaker, first "dry-shake" the ingredients without the ice. This will create the desired silky texture. Then add the ice and shake until the drink is chilled.

GINGER LIME WHISKEY SOUR

In the mid-1800s, sailors commonly brought citrus fruits (lemons, limes, oranges) as well as alcohol (whiskey, bourbon, rum) on board with them, especially on long voyages. Fresh drinking water was scarce, and the combination of whiskey and citrus was perfect for quenching thirst. In this version of the classic cocktail, ginger adds a spicy kick.

GLASS: Lowball	GARNISH: Candied ginger, lime wedge
2 oz/60 ml bourbon ½ oz/15 ml Ginger-Honey Syrup (page 63) 1½ oz/45 ml lime juice, freshly squeezed	1 egg white (see Tip, page 85) Candied ginger, for garnish Lime wedge, for garnish

In a cocktail shaker, add the bourbon, Ginger-Honey Syrup, lime juice, and egg white. Shake until frothy. Add ice and shake until chilled. Strain into a cocktail glass with ice and garnish with candied ginger and a lime wedge.

COSMOPOLITAN

May 7 is National Cosmopolitan Day, so pull out the cocktail shaker and let's have at it! Created in the 1980s, the Cosmo has risen in stature to be called a classic, especially since it was the drink of choice in the TV show Sex and the City. *The original drink was meant to be tart—the cranberry juice is there for the color—so feel free to experiment. The possibilities are endless.*

GLASS: Martini		GARNISH: Orange twist
1½ oz/45 ml citrus vodka ½ oz/15 ml Cointreau ½ oz/15 ml cranberry juice		⅓ oz/10 ml lime juice, freshly squeezed Orange twist, for garnish

In a cocktail shaker, add the vodka, Cointreau, cranberry juice, and lime juice. Add ice and shake until chilled. Strain into a cocktail glass and garnish with an orange twist.

VARIATION: *The* FRENCH COSMOPOLITAN *substitutes in Grand Marnier for the orange liqueur. In a cocktail shaker, add 1½ oz/45 ml citrus vodka, ½ oz (15 ml) Grand Marnier, ½ oz (15 ml) cranberry juice, and ⅓ oz (10 ml) lime juice. Add ice and shake until chilled. Strain into a cocktail glass and garnish with an orange twist.*

SPICY PALOMA

A close cousin of the Margarita, the Paloma is wildly popular in Mexico. This spicy version is just as refreshing and easy to make as the original. If you want an even spicier finish, combine equal parts salt and Tajín seasoning, then pour the mixture onto a small plate. Rub the rim of a cocktail glass with a lime wedge and dip it into the mixture.

GLASS: Highball	GARNISH: Grapefruit wheel

2 oz/60 ml tequila blanco

2 oz/60 ml grapefruit juice, freshly squeezed

½ oz/15 ml lime juice, freshly squeezed

¼ oz/7 ml Spiced Agave Syrup (page 93)

2 oz/60 ml sparkling water

Grapefruit wheel, for garnish

In a chilled cocktail glass with ice, add the tequila, grapefruit juice, lime juice, and Spiced Agave Syrup. Stir until chilled and top with sparkling water. Garnish with a grapefruit wheel.

RECIPE

Spiced Agave Syrup

1 cup/340 g agave
nectar

1 whole dried pepper
(ancho or guajillo)

In a medium saucepan over medium
heat, combine the agave nectar, 1 cup
(240 ml) of water, and dried pepper.
Bring to a boil and let simmer, about
5 minutes. Remove from the heat and
let cool. Strain and discard the pepper.
Store in an airtight container in the
refrigerator for up to two weeks.

CHRYSANTHEMUM

This drink is among the oft-forgotten vermouth-based cocktails from the Prohibition era. But try it once, and you won't forget it! Having no base liquor, the Chrysanthemum is well suited for any time you just want a low-alcohol drink. And, while any dry vermouth will work, Noilly Prat Extra Dry provides a slightly sweeter finish and a beautiful, golden color.

GLASS: Coupe	GARNISH: Orange twist

Absinthe, to rinse

2 oz/60 ml dry vermouth

½ oz/15 ml Bénédictine

Orange twist, for garnish

In a cocktail glass, add a splash of absinthe, swirl to coat the inside, and pour out the excess. In a mixing glass filled with ice, add the vermouth and Bénédictine. Stir until well chilled. Strain into the prepared cocktail glass and garnish with an orange twist.

GIBSON MARTINI

Are you getting bored of martini variations yet? Hopefully not, because this one truly is delicious.

GLASS: Coupe		GARNISH: Cocktail onions

2½ oz/75 ml gin

½ oz/15 ml dry vermouth

Cocktail onions, for garnish

In a mixing glass filled with ice, add the gin and vermouth. Stir until well chilled. Strain into a cocktail glass and garnish with cocktail onions.

PEACH-RASPBERRY BELLINI

The Bellini cocktail dates back to 1948. The founder and barman of Harry's Bar in Venice (one of Ernest Hemingway's favorite haunts) drew inspiration from the local produce, especially the peaches, as well as the famed sparkling wines. This version of the drink adds raspberry for a nice twist on the original.

GLASS: Champagne flute	GARNISH: Peach slice

1½ oz/45 ml Peach-Raspberry Purée (page 101)
4 oz/120 ml prosecco
Peach slice, for garnish

In a Champagne flute, add the Peach-Raspberry Purée and top with prosecco. Garnish with a peach slice.

RECIPE

Peach-Raspberry Purée

1 peach, peeled, pitted, and diced

8 fresh raspberries

In a blender, combine the peaches, raspberries, and ¼ cup (60 ml) of water and blend until smooth. Pour the mixture through a fine-mesh sieve to remove large pieces. Store the strained purée in the refrigerator up to four weeks.

AVIATION

Crème de violette is what gives this drink its steely purple color. However, the amount of crème de violette is a point of contention. Here's a thought: Try using an indigo gin, which will balance the floral flavors of this cocktail. It will lend a more vibrant purple color.

GLASS: Coupe	GARNISH: Brandied cherry

2 oz/60 ml dry gin

½ oz/15 ml maraschino liqueur (see Tip, page 37)

¼ oz/7 ml crème de violette

¾ oz/22 ml lemon juice, freshly squeezed

Brandied cherry, for garnish

In a cocktail shaker, add the gin, maraschino liqueur, crème de violette, and lemon juice. Add ice and shake until chilled. Strain into a cocktail glass and garnish with a brandied cherry.

VARIATION: *The **MOONLIGHT** cocktail, invented by legendary barman Gary "Gaz" Regan, is a delightful twist on the Aviation. To make it, swap in Cointreau for the maraschino liqueur and use lime juice instead of lemon.*

CLOVER CLUB

Originating at the Clover Club in Brooklyn, this pretty pink cocktail is a delicious throwback to old-school New York. Perfect for sipping on a warm spring day, the Clover Club is a classic example of the pre–Prohibition era's cocktail culture and is still widely enjoyed today for its light and refreshing taste.

GLASS: Coupe	GARNISH: Raspberries

3 oz/90 ml gin

¾ oz/22 ml Raspberry Syrup (page 107)

1 oz/30 ml lemon juice, freshly squeezed

1 egg white (see Tip, page 85)

Raspberries, for garnish

In a cocktail shaker, add the gin, Raspberry Syrup, lemon juice, and egg white. Shake until frothy and well combined. Add ice and shake until chilled. Double-strain into a cocktail glass and garnish with raspberries.

RECIPE

Raspberry Syrup

1 cup/120 g raspberries

1 cup/200 g sugar

In a medium saucepan over medium heat, combine the raspberries, sugar, and 1 cup (240 ml) of water. Bring to a boil and stir to dissolve the sugar, about 5 minutes. Remove from the heat and let cool. Strain and discard the raspberries. Store in an airtight container in the refrigerator for up to two weeks.

MINT JULEP

As the official drink of the Kentucky Derby, the Mint Julep has a rich history. Its popularity has made it a staple of Southern cuisine and a symbol of Southern hospitality.

GLASS: Julep cup	GARNISH: Mint sprig

10 fresh mint leaves
½ oz/15 ml simple syrup
2½ oz/75 ml bourbon
Mint sprig, for garnish

In a metal julep cup, add the mint leaves and simple syrup and lightly muddle to release the mint oils. Add the bourbon and stir. Pack the cup with crushed ice, then garnish with a sprig of mint.

LAVENDER BEE'S KNEES

The "bee's knees" phrase dates back to the 1920s, when flappers compared anything that was the best or the finest to a part of an animal. (Let's bring back the "flea's eyebrows.") Numerous expressions like this arose in that era, though few stood the test of time. In this recipe, the addition of lavender to the honey simple syrup adds a floral note to the traditional gin sour.

GLASS: Coupe		GARNISH: Lemon peel

2 oz/60 ml gin

¾ oz/22 ml lemon juice, freshly squeezed

½ oz/15 ml Honey-Lavender Syrup (page 113)

Lemon peel, for garnish

In a cocktail shaker, add the gin, lemon juice, and Honey-Lavender Syrup. Add ice and shake until chilled. Strain into a cocktail glass and garnish with a lemon peel.

Honey-Lavender Syrup

¼ cup/85 g honey   1 Tbsp lavender

In a small saucepan over medium heat, combine the honey, ¼ cup (60 ml) of water, and the lavender. Bring to a boil and stir until the honey is dissolved and the lavender is fragrant, 2 to 3 minutes. Remove from the heat and let cool. Store in an airtight container in the refrigerator for up to two weeks.

LEMON DROP

Pucker up! This deceptively simple drink knows how to sweet talk. Born in the hippie heyday of 1970s San Francisco, this lemon-laced libation is the perfect balance of sour and sweet.

GLASS: Coupe or martini	GARNISH: Lemon peel

Sugar, for the rim

Lemon wedge, for the rim

2 oz/60 ml vodka

½ oz/15 ml triple sec

1 oz/30 ml lemon juice, freshly squeezed

¾ oz/22 ml simple syrup

Lemon peel, for garnish

To prepare the cocktail glass, sprinkle sugar onto a small plate. Wipe a lemon wedge around the edge of a cocktail glass, then dip the rim into the sugar.

In a cocktail shaker, add the vodka, triple sec, lemon juice, and simple syrup. Add ice and shake until chilled. Strain into the prepared cocktail glass and garnish with a lemon peel.

SUMMER

Gin & Tonic   118

Dirty Shirley   121

Aperol Spritz   122

Mojito   125

Mai Tai   126

Blue Hawaiian   130

Tequila Sunrise   133

Apricot Daiquiri   134

Hot Mango Margarita   137

Piña Colada   138

Necromancer   142

Summer Shandy   145

Paper Plane   146

GIN & TONIC

In the eighteenth century, British officers stationed in India were given rations of quinine to treat malaria. Quinine is quite bitter, however, so the officers mixed it with tonic water, as well as sugar and lime. The British, being ever-so-civilized, of course also gave the officers a ration of gin. (You know where this is going, right?)

GLASS: Highball	GARNISH: Lime wedge

2 oz/60 ml gin
¾ oz/22 ml lime juice, freshly squeezed
4 oz/120 ml tonic water
Lime wedge, for garnish

In a cocktail glass filled with ice, add the gin and lime juice. Stir to combine. Top with the tonic water and garnish with a lime wheel.

VARIATION: *For a colorful flair, try using a naturally dyed gin. Contemporary distillers offer numerous options, ranging from pink to purple to indigo.*

DIRTY SHIRLEY

This bright-red drink harkens back to the days when parents thought serving the kids a fake cocktail was cool. (Ah, good ol' Mom and Dad raising the kids right.) Our version—with alcohol, clearly—adds a bit of sophistication by using Pomegranate Syrup instead of grenadine.

GLASS: Highball		GARNISH: Maraschino cherry

2 oz/60 ml vodka

1 oz/30 ml Pomegranate Syrup (page 31)

8 oz/240 ml lemon-lime soda

Maraschino cherry, for garnish

In a cocktail glass filled with ice, add the vodka and Pomegranate Syrup and stir to mix. Fill the glass with the lemon-lime soda and top with a maraschino cherry.

VARIATION: **CLASSIC SHIRLEY TEMPLE.** *In a cocktail glass filled with ice, add 1 oz (30 ml) Pomegranate Syrup. Then top with 4 oz (120 ml) each of lemon-lime soda and ginger ale and stir to mix. Garnish with a maraschino cherry.*

APEROL SPRITZ

This cheerful, bright "sunset in a glass" is the embodiment of summer. It has a low alcohol content, meaning a spritz or two will whet your appetite perfectly for dinner. Is there a better way to relax after a long workweek? Doubtful.

GLASS: Wineglass	GARNISH: Orange wheel

2 oz/60 ml Aperol

1 oz/30 ml soda water

3 oz/90 ml prosecco

Orange wheel, for garnish

In a wineglass filled with ice, add the Aperol and sparkling water. Top with prosecco and garnish with an orange wheel.

VARIATION: *If you want a more intense flavor, try a* **CAMPARI SPRITZ**. *Like its cousin, it follows the same "3-2-1" ratio of ingredients, swapping Campari for the Aperol.*

MOJITO

Whether you make a single drink or a pitcher, a Mojito is the perfect drink for hot summer afternoons. Be careful with that pitcher—you might be tempted to drink it all.

GLASS: Highball	GARNISH: Mint leaves, lime wheel
5 fresh mint leaves, plus more for garnish 1 lime, cut into wedges 2 Tbsp sugar	1½ oz/45 ml white rum ½ cup/120 ml soda water Lime wheel, for garnish

In a sturdy cocktail glass, add the mint and lightly muddle to release the mint oils. Add the lime wedges and sugar, and continue muddling to release the lime juice. Fill the glass with ice, then add the rum. Finish by adding the soda water. Stir to mix and garnish with more mint leaves and a lime wheel.

VARIATION: *Try making Mojitos with fresh watermelon or strawberries. Again, begin by lightly muddling the mint. Next add the limes wedges and sugar along with the fresh fruit and continue muddling. Fill the glass with ice, add the rum, and top with soda water.*

MAI TAI

This mainstay of tiki bars everywhere is also the perfect beach cocktail. Developed in the mid-1940s in Oakland, California, this cocktail was meant to quickly transport you to the tropics. Loosely translated from Tahitian, Mai Tai means "out of this world."

GLASS: Coupe or Lowball	GARNISH: Lime wheel

1½ oz/45 ml white rum

¾ oz/22 ml curaçao (see Tip, page 129)

¾ oz/22 ml lime juice, freshly squeezed

½ oz/15 ml orgeat

½ oz/15 ml dark rum

Lime wheel, for garnish

In a cocktail shaker, add the white rum, curaçao, lime juice, and orgeat. Add ice and shake until chilled. Strain into a cocktail glass with ice and pour the dark rum over the top. Garnish with a lime wheel.

TIP

Curaçao

Curaçao, an orange liqueur, can be hard to find. If you need a substitute, try Grand Marnier or Cointreau. (Blue curaçao has added dye coloring.)

BLUE HAWAIIAN

Tiki bar calling your name? Here's something fun and refreshing . . . and a bit out of the ordinary. You may just want to invite some friends over for this one.

GLASS: Highball or hurricane	GARNISH: Pineapple wedge, maraschino cherry

1½ oz/45 ml white rum

¾ oz/22 ml blue curaçao (see Tip, page 129)

2 oz/60 ml pineapple juice

¾ oz/22 ml cream of coconut (see Tip, page 141)

Pineapple wedge, for garnish

Maraschino cherry, for garnish

In a cocktail shaker, add the rum, curaçao, pineapple juice, and cream of coconut. Add ice and shake until chilled. Strain into a cocktail glass with ice and garnish with a pineapple wedge and maraschino cherry.

TEQUILA SUNRISE

The key to this simple drink is to slowly add the Pomegranate Syrup at the end. The syrup is heavier than the other ingredients and will sink in the glass. Don't stir, or your sunrise will become foggy. If you order this cocktail in a bar, it will likely be made with grenadine, which has a more electric color. Feel free to use either.

GLASS: Highball or hurricane		GARNISH: Dried orange slice, maraschino cherry
2 oz/60 ml tequila blanco 4 oz orange juice, freshly squeezed ¼ oz/7 ml Pomegranate Syrup (page 31)		Dried orange slice, for garnish (see Tip, page 17) Maraschino cherry, for garnish

In a cocktail glass filled with ice, combine the tequila and orange juice and stir to mix. Slowly pour the Pomegranate Syrup around the edge of the glass. The syrup will sink to the bottom and then slowly rise. Garnish with an orange slice and maraschino cherry.

VARIATION: *Substitute grapefruit juice for the orange juice and you have a* **TEQUILA SUNSET**. (The book is called *Friday Night Cocktails*, after all.)

APRICOT DAIQUIRI

Daiquiris are known for their fresh fruit possibilities, and this version doesn't disappoint. The hint of apricot flavor truly is a remarkable change of pace.

GLASS: Daiquiri or Margarita	GARNISH: Apricot slice

2 apricots, sliced

1 oz/30 ml simple syrup

2 oz/60 ml white rum

1 oz/30 ml lime juice, freshly squeezed

Apricot slice, for garnish

In a cocktail shaker, add the apricots and simple syrup and muddle until well combined. Then add the rum and lime juice. Add ice and shake until chilled. Double-strain into a cocktail glass with ice and garnish with a slice of apricot.

VARIATION: *To make a* **FROZEN APRICOT DAIQUIRI**, *add all cocktail ingredients to a blender with ½ cup of ice and ½ oz (15 ml) simple syrup. Blend until completely smooth, about 1 minute with no large chunks remaining. Pour into a cocktail glass.*

HOT MANGO MARGARITA

The addition of jalapeño to this (or any) margarita will surely grab your attention. You may need to experiment with mango juice vs. mango nectar, however. Both are readily available. Mango juice is made of 100 percent mangoes and is less sweet than mango nectar.

GLASS: Margarita or lowball		GARNISH: Mango slice

Tajín seasoning, for the rim

Lime wedge, for the rim

1 jalapeño pepper, seeded and sliced

1 oz/30 ml lime juice, freshly squeezed

4 oz/120 ml mango juice

2 oz/60 ml tequila blanco

1 oz/30 ml Cointreau

Mango slice, for garnish

To prepare the cocktail glass, sprinkle Tajín seasoning onto a small plate. Wipe a lime wedge around the edge of a margarita glass, then dip the rim into the Tajín seasoning.

In a cocktail shaker, add the jalapeño and the lime juice, and muddle to release the jalapeño oils. Then add the mango juice, tequila, and Cointreau. Add ice and shake until chilled. Strain into the prepared cocktail glass with ice and garnish with a mango slice.

PIÑA COLADA

The national drink of Puerto Rico, the Piña Colada is as delicious as it is easy to make. The best part is that its ingredients are incredibly versatile. Try substituting fresh pineapple (freeze the chunks, then blend them into juice); coconut milk (a less-sweet option than cream of coconut); and adding a squeeze of lime juice. Often found mixed in a blender, this version is shaken over ice.

GLASS: Highball or hurricane	GARNISH: Pineapple wedge, maraschino cherry

2 oz/60 ml white rum

2 oz/60 ml pineapple juice

1½ oz/45 ml cream of coconut (see Tip, page 141)

Pineapple wedge, for garnish

Maraschino cherry, for garnish

In a cocktail shaker, add the rum, pineapple juice, and cream of coconut. Add ice and shake until chilled. Strain into a cocktail glass with ice. Garnish with a pineapple wedge and maraschino cherry.

Cream of Coconut vs. Coconut Cream

Don't confuse cream of coconut with coconut cream. The two are not interchangeable. Cream of coconut has added sugar, whereas coconut cream is just made of unsweetened coconut.

NECROMANCER

It may be time to bring absinthe out of the shadows. Long thought to cause hallucinations and even madness, this potent alcohol was banned across Europe and the United States for nearly a century. (The U.S. lifted its ban in 2007.) Today, because of its intense flavor, many drinks call for just a rinse. The Necromancer shows that the spirit is certainly worthy of a place at the table.

GLASS: Coupe	GARNISH: Lemon twist

¾ oz/22 ml absinthe

¾ oz/22 ml elderflower liqueur

¾ oz/22 ml Lillet Blanc

¾ oz/22 ml lemon juice, freshly squeezed

1 dash London dry gin

Lemon twist, for garnish

In a cocktail shaker, add the absinthe, elderflower liqueur, Lillet Blanc, lemon juice, and gin. Add ice and shake until chilled. Strain into a cocktail glass and garnish with a lemon twist.

SUMMER SHANDY

Similar to making a wine spritzer by combining your favorite wine with sparkling water, a shandy combines beer with sparkling lemonade. It's that simple. For the beer, choose either a hefeweizen, pilsner, or pale ale. Okay, maybe it's not a cocktail per se, but the shandy certainly is refreshing.

GLASS: Beer glass	GARNISH: Lemon slice
6 oz/180 ml beer 6 oz/180 ml sparkling lemonade Lemon slice, for garnish	
In a beer glass, combine the beer and lemonade. Garnish with the lemon slice.	

PAPER PLANE

Created in 2008 by New York City bartender Sam Ross, the Paper Plane is a riff on the Last Word (page 34). Although at first glance the drinks seem quite different, both are composed of equal parts alcohol, two liqueurs, and citrus. Ross's goal was to create a delicious concoction using readily available ingredients and that was easily made. Indeed, no special syrups and no garnishes necessary.

GLASS: Coupe	GARNISH: None

¾ oz/22 ml bourbon

¾ oz/22 ml Amaro Nonino

¾ oz/22 ml Aperol

¾ oz/22 ml lemon juice, freshly squeezed

In a cocktail shaker, add the bourbon, amaro, Aperol, and lemon juice. Add ice and shake until chilled. Strain into a cocktail glass.

VARIATION: *Although it's purely for show, the original Paper Plane cocktail was garnished with a tiny, folded paper plane. If you're have a particularly slow Friday night, give it a try!*

Index

50/50 Martini, 71

A

absinthe, 20, 94, 142

agave nectar, 76, 93

amaretto liqueur, 15

Amaretto Sour, 15

Amaro Averna, 49

Amaro Nonino, 146

Aperol, 122, 146

Aperol Spritz, 122

applejack, 41, 83

Applejack Sour, 41

Apricot Daiquiri, 134

Aviation, 102

B

barware, 10

beer, 145

Bénédictine, 94

bitters
    Angostura, 27, 41, 49, 50, 54
    chocolate, 23
    Peychaud's, 20
    orange, 28, 49, 54, 71

black currant liqueur, 42

Black Manhattan, 49

Blood Orange Margarita, 76

Blue Hawaiian, 130

Boulevardier, 75

bourbon, 15, 23, 54, 57, 64, 72, 75, 86, 108, 146

Bradsell, Dick, 58

brandy, 45

Buttered Rum Batter, 67, 69

C

Campari, 38, 75, 122

Campari Spritz, 122

Champagne, 42, 64

Chocolate Old Fashioned, 23

Chrysanthemum, 94

citrus, dried, 17

Classic Manhattan, 49

Classic Negroni, 38

Classic Shirley Temple, 121

Clementine Wallbanger, 54

Clover Club, 105

coconut cream, 141

coconut, cream of, 130, 138, 141

coffee, 58, 72

coffee liqueur, 58

cognac, 20

Cointreau, 45, 89, 102, 137

Cosmopolitan, 89

Cranberry Mule, 53

Cranberry Mule Mocktail, 53

crème de violette, 102

Cucumber Mint Gimlet, 80

curaçao, 126, 129, 130

D

Dirty Martini, 71

Dirty Shirley, 121

E

Easy Espresso Martini, 58

egg white, 15, 83, 85, 86, 105

elderflower liqueur, 17, 64, 142

espresso, 58

Espresso Martini, 58

F

fernet, 27

French 75, 64

French 76, 64

French 77, 64

French 95, 64

French Cosmopolitan, 89

French Pear Martini, 17

Frozen Apricot Daiquiri, 134

G

Galliano liqueur, 54

Galliano Old Fashioned, 54

Gibson Martini, 97

gin, 24, 27, 34, 38, 64, 71, 80, 83, 97, 102, 105, 111, 118, 142

Gin & Tonic, 118

ginger, 63

ginger beer, 53

Ginger-Honey Syrup, 61, 63, 86

Ginger Lime Whiskey Sour, 86

Ginger Simple Syrup

glassware, 11

Grand Marnier, 89

Green Chartreuse, 34

H

Hanky Panky, 27

honey, 57, 63, 69, 113

Honey-Lavender Syrup, 111, 113

Hot Buttered Rum, 67

Hot Mango Margarita, 137

Hot Toddy, 57

I

Irish Coffee, 72

Irish whiskey, 72

J

Jack Rose, 41

Kentucky Coffee, 72

Kir Royale, 42

L

La última palabra, 34

Last Word, 34

Lavender Bee's Knees, 111

Lemon Drop, 114

Lillet Blanc, 24, 142

M

Mai Tai, 126

maple syrup, 33, 41

maraschino liqueur, 27, 34, 37, 102

Martinez, 27

mezcal, 34

Mint Julep, 108

Mojito, 125

Moonlight, 102

Morganthaler, Jeffrey, 15

N

Necromancer, 142

Negroni Sbagliato, 38

O

Old Fashioned, 23

orgeat, 126

P

Paper Plane, 146

Peach-Raspberry Bellini, 98

Peach-Raspberry Purée, 98, 101

Pear & Elderflower Sparkler, 17

Penicillin, 61

Perfect Rob Roy, 50

Piña Colada, 138

Pink Lady, 83

Pomegranate Syrup, 28, 31, 41, 83, 121, 133

prosecco, 17, 38, 98, 122

Pumpkin Pie Cocktail, 33

Pumpkin Pie Mule, 33

pumpkin pie spice, 33

pumpkin purée, 33

R

Raspberry Syrup, 105, 107

Regan, Gary "Gaz," 102

Rob Roy, 50

Ross, Sam, 61

Rum
    dark, 33
    gold, 67
    white, 125, 126, 130, 138

rye whiskey, 20, 28, 41, 49

S

Sazerac, 20

Scofflaw, 28

Scotch whisky, 50, 61

Sidecar, 45

simple syrup, 15, 58, 64, 80, 108, 114

Smith, Todd, 49

Spiced Agave Syrup, 90, 93

Spicy Paloma, 90

Summer Shandy, 145

T

tequila blanco, 76, 90, 133, 137

Tequila Sunrise, 133

Tequila Sunset, 133

triple sec, 114

V

vanilla extract, 33

vermouth
    dry, 28, 50, 71, 94, 97
    sweet, 27, 38, 49, 50, 75

Vesper Martini, 24

Vodka, 17, 24, 33, 53, 54, 64, 71, 89, 114, 121

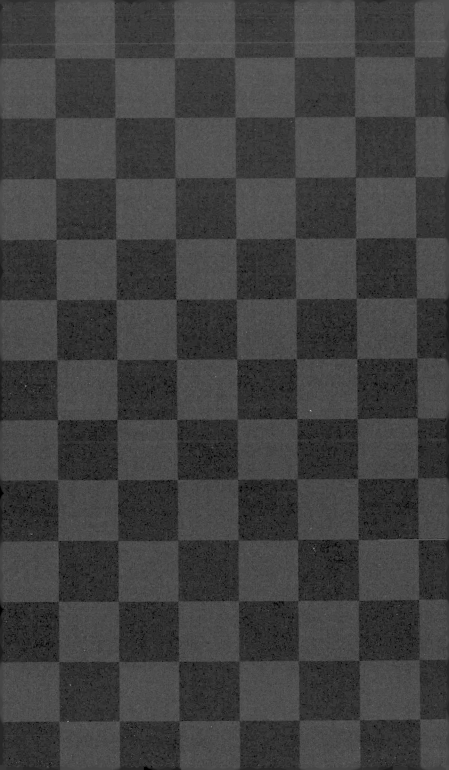